WILD BIRD GUIDES

Red-tailed Hawk

Author/Publisher's Note: The photograph on the right-hand side of page 13 depicts an immature Cooper's Hawk, not an immature Red-tailed Hawk, as indicated. The accompanying text describing the red-tail is correct.

0 11557 02914 7

WILD BIRD GUIDES
Red-tailed Hawk

Charles R. Preston

STACKPOLE
BOOKS

Published by
STACKPOLE BOOKS
5067 Ritter Road
Mechanicsburg, PA 17055
www.stackpolebooks.com

Printed in China

10 9 8 7 6 5 4 3 2 1

First edition

Cover photo by Laura Riley

Library of Congress Cataloging-in-Publication Data

Preston, Charles R.
    Red-tailed hawk / Charles R. Preston. — 1st ed.
        p.   cm. — (Wild bird guides)
    Includes bibliographical references.
    ISBN 0-8117-2914-1 (alk. paper)
    1. Red-tailed hawk.   I. Title.   II. Series.
QL692.F32P74   2000
598.9'44—dc21
                                                                    99-35582
                                                                    CIP

For my father, Charles M. Preston,
for giving me dreams

my mother, Mary Breedlove Preston,
for showing me how to pursue my dreams

my mate, Penny Hatcher Preston,
for sharing dreams
and keeping them alive

Contents

Portrait of a Generalist

The key to the broad distribution and sweeping success of the Red-tailed Hawk in North America lies in its ability to tolerate a wide range of conditions and exploit a wide range of resources. In ecological parlance, such an animal is termed a generalist. Of course, *generalist* is a comparative rather than an absolute term. It is most appropriately used to compare two species with respect to their use of specific resources. Nonetheless, the Red-tailed Hawk merits this sweeping designation and deserves to wear the "jack-of-all-trades, master-of-none" crown among diurnal, or day-active, raptors in North America. This book is a portrait and celebration of this magnificent generalist.

The dramatic sight and sound of a soaring Red-tailed Hawk are familiar icons of wildness across North America. Whenever Hollywood wants to evoke a sense of the great outdoors, you can bet that you will hear the piercing *kee-eee-arrrr* of a Red-tailed Hawk in the background. More often than not, it is the robust call of a red-tail you hear when an eagle is shown on film.

For most Americans, whether raised in urban, suburban, or rural environments, the Red-tailed Hawk is the first raptor, or bird of prey, they encounter. This large hawk ranges through most of North America—from Alaska through northern Canada to Labrador, south to Mexico and the West Indies—and occupies a great variety of open and semiopen habitats.

Red-tails are usually conspicuous wherever they occur, habitually perching on roadside fence posts and utility poles. This young bird, with a bulging crop, has evidently just returned to a favorite roadside perch after finishing a meal.

In wooded areas of eastern North America, the red-tail is a common sight perched high in a tree, often far out on a limb.

The Red-tailed Hawk is a member of the bird order Falconiformes, which includes all the diurnal raptors. These birds, including eagles, hawks, kites, falcons, and their allies, share many physical traits that aid them in hunting and killing other animals for food.

A raptor's leg muscles are extremely strong, and the feet possess four long, curved, sharp talons for capturing and disabling prey. The tough scales on the feet of the Red-tailed Hawk help protect the lower extremities from the bites and scratches of struggling prey. The talons are composed of bone encased in a hard sheath of keratin. The longest talon is found on the hind toe, or hallux. The hallux is the bird counterpart of the human big toe. Many a careless researcher has suffered a painful injury as a result of being seized by the talons of a captive hawk. Great care must be taken even when banding raptor nestlings.

A typical raptor bill is strongly hooked and extremely sharp for tearing flesh. The point is needle-sharp, and the shearing edges along the sides of the upper bill act as knife blades, slicing off bits of flesh brought up to them by the lower bill. The fleshy covering at the base of the beak is called a cere. All diurnal raptors possess a cere, and its color may play a significant role in signaling age and physical condition in some species. Typically, the cere is light green in young Red-tailed Hawks but changes to bright yellow with age.

The large eyes of a raptor are positioned on the front of the face, affording binocular vision and excellent depth perception. If our eyes were as large in proportion to our bodies as the eyes of a Red-tailed Hawk, they would be about the size of tennis balls.

Eye color varies among raptor species and may change with age. In Red-tailed Hawks, eye color is somewhat variable. Young birds, like the one below left, often have light brown or yellowish eyes.

The red-tail below right exhibits the deep brown eyes typical of older birds. Each eye is protected by a ring of bone and moves only slightly in its socket. Thus, a raptor must move its entire head to change its viewing perspective. A flexible neck allows the head to move through an extremely wide range of motion. It's the next best thing to having eyes in the back of its head.

Above each eye is a protective bony extension of the skull, called the supraorbital ridge. This prominent feature adds significantly to a raptor's seemingly intense demeanor. Muscles surrounding the eye function to change the shape of the eye lens and allow the raptor to rapidly change focus between objects near and far. An abundance of sensory cells in the retina of the raptor eye allows these birds to see greater detail at greater distances than can humans. Special oil droplets present in the eyes of all birds may aid them in discriminating objects from similarly colored backgrounds. All in all, the scene apparent to a Red-tailed Hawk as it surveys the environment must be utterly luxurious in color and detail compared with what a human would perceive.

The Red-tailed Hawk belongs to the genus *Buteo*, a group of stout-bodied, broad-winged raptors. Some twenty-seven species of hawks are assigned to this genus worldwide, including representatives in Africa, Eurasia, the Galápagos Islands, Hawaii, and Madagascar, as well as South, Central, and North America. Some other fairly widespread buteos in North America include the Red-shouldered Hawk, Broad-winged Hawk, Ferruginous Hawk, Swainson's Hawk, and Rough-legged Hawk. With practice, buteos can be distinguished from other North American raptors on the basis of size and shape. This red-tail can be recognized as a buteo by its distinctive silhouette alone. The buteos are somewhat smaller than eagles but are decidedly stocky.

When viewed from below, a soaring buteo has long, broad wings and typically displays a relatively short, broad, fan-shaped tail.

The average Red-tailed Hawk weighs a little more than 2 pounds (about 1,100 grams), is roughly 18 to 25 inches (455 to 635 millimeters) in length from the tip of the beak to the tip of the longest tail feather, and sports a wingspan of just over 4 feet (1.2 meters). As in most falconiformes, females are somewhat larger than males. Other North American buteos are similar to the red-tail in size but differ in a variety of plumage characteristics. Ultimate success in field identification depends on the view provided by the hawk and the experience of the observer.

Complicating matters is the fact that the red-tail, like many of its relatives, is highly variable in plumage color. The variation is extreme in some red-tail populations, especially in the western Great Plains, Rocky Mountain, and Great Basin regions. In these populations, ventral plumage coloration may vary among individuals from nearly white to deep chocolate or reddish brown to sooty black. A situation like this, in which two or more distinct, genetically determined forms occur in one interbreeding population, is termed polymorphism. The various forms are termed morphs, and the variation is independent of age or gender. Light morphs far outnumber the other morphs in most polymorphic red-tail populations. In the field, it is often difficult to distinguish dark red-tail morphs from dark morphs of other buteos.

No satisfactory explanation for the widespread occurrence of polymorphism in buteos is available. Comparing the behavior and ecology of the morphs may offer some clues. Several years ago, I conducted a study of Red-tailed Hawks overwintering in northwestern Arkansas. Many birds that breed farther north and west spend the winter in this part of the country, so I had the opportunity to observe an abundance of red-tails of light, dark, and intermediate morphs. I found that light morphs tended to perch in the open, often near the tops of trees or other structures, whereas dark morphs more frequently perched in groups of trees where branches were more dense. Thus dark birds perched against a relatively dark background, and light birds perched against a relatively light one. The birds seemingly selected perch sites that afforded the greatest personal concealment, but whether this differential perchsite selection between dark and light birds is related to hunting success or survivorship remains a mystery.

The distinguishing characteristic of the typical Red-tailed Hawk adult, whether a light or dark morph, is the visually striking brick red tail. Although they are missing in this bird, several thin, dark bands may be present, especially in western birds. A slightly wider subterminal band, faintly visible here, is almost always present.

In light morphs, the top of the head and back of the body are dark brown, with some small whitish and buffy patches forming a V visible between the shoulders in most perched individuals.

The front of the body is typically whitish, and a stippled dark band is usually evident across the abdomen in most races. This belly band is highly variable, however, and is not a reliable characteristic for identification. The throat in eastern red-tails is typically white, but it may be dark, even in light morphs, in individuals from other regions.

The lower extremities are feathered only about halfway to the feet, so a good portion of the bare, yellow legs is usually visible. Feathers on the upper legs may be immaculate, as in this case, or spotted with dark brown.

In flight, most light and intermediate red-tail morphs can be identified by the presence of a distinctive dark brown patch along the leading edge of the wing close to the body. That mark is accented in many birds by a dark comma- or C-shaped mark at the base of the leading primary feathers. The tips of the primaries are dark.

Swainson's and Ferruginous hawks are two similarly sized close relatives that share the open range with red-tails in the western United States and Canada. Like the red-tail, each is polymorphic, with light morphs far more common than darker birds. Adult light-morph Swainson's Hawks (left) typically sport a deep orange-brown bib on the upper breast and an unmarked, whitish belly. The underside of each wing is two-toned, with the leading edge light and the trailing edge dark. The tail is gray-brown, with several thin, dark bands of equal thickness, in addition to a wider subterminal band. As in Red-tailed Hawks, the legs of Swainson's Hawks are feathered only about halfway to the feet. The tail of an adult Ferruginous Hawk (right) may be white, gray, pale red, or a combination and typically has no banding. The underparts of light morphs are white but can be marked with rufous streaks or bars. The back is usually much redder than that of the red-tail. The leg feathers of adult Ferruginous Hawks are typically rufous, and when seen from below they form a dark **V**. The legs are feathered all the way to the feet.

Juvenile birds of all North American buteos look much alike. The underparts are typically streaked with varying amounts of brown. The tails are also brown with many narrow, dark bands. The young red-tail contortionist at left has paused to tend to some unruly wing feathers.

Probably the best characteristic for identifying juvenile red-tails in the field is a pale patch appearing in the outer half of the upper surface of the wing, just visible in the lower portion of the photograph at right.

Polymorphism is a major source of variation in appearance within some populations of the Red-tailed Hawk. There is also some variation among geographic populations, or races. The Red-tailed Hawk population breeding at the extreme northwestern limits of the range, in northwestern Canada and Alaska, is referred to as Harlan's Red-tailed Hawk. It is so different in some aspects of its appearance from other red-tail races that it was once considered a distinct species. A Harlan's red-tail is typically very dark above and below and has a reddish tail mottled with longitudinal streaks or bars of gray, white, and dark brown. There are also some light-breasted birds in this population.

Most Harlan's Red-tailed Hawks migrate south for the winter and may be seen as far east as Tennessee and as far south as Texas and Louisiana.

In contrast to the dark Harlan's Red-tailed Hawks, many birds breeding in the upper Midwest, including parts of North Dakota, eastern Montana, and southern Alberta and Saskatchewan, are very pale in plumage color. These birds are referred to as Krider's Red-tailed Hawks. A typical Krider's red-tail, like the one shown here, gives the appearance of a faded or lightly bleached version of the typical Red-tailed Hawk from eastern North America.

One of the most strikingly beautiful birds I have ever observed was an albinistic Red-tailed Hawk with an immaculate, snow white head and body and a bright red tail save for two white tail feathers. Albinism, the lack of pigmentation, may occur in any bird species. It is more commonly observed in red-tails than in most other raptors. Albinism may affect all or part of the body. Thus, some albinistic red-tails may exhibit a mosaic of white and normal plumage and possess pigmented eyes, talons, and bill.

Others, like the ghostly bird at right, are entirely white. Sight and, therefore, chances of long-term survival are generally better in birds with pigmented eyes.

Like other buteos, Red-tailed-Hawks spend most daylight hours perching in a site that provides them with a generous view of the surrounding countryside. Red-tails are patient, sit-and-wait hunters and thus are ever on the alert for the slightest movement of potential prey.

Generally shy in nature, a Red-tailed Hawk may flush from a perch when approached within 100 yards by a human on foot. In contrast, these birds quickly learn to tolerate moving vehicles in close proximity to roadside perches.

Besides functioning as a hunting station, a perch also serves as a convenient grooming site. The red-tail uses its bill to collect oil, produced by the uropygial gland at the base of the tail, and to meticulously preen its feathers, one by one. During a preening session, the feathers are often partially erected, giving the hawk a fluffy, almost comical appearance. Frequently, the entire plumage is shaken vigorously before being smoothed back into place. Preening is an important activity that helps waterproof the plumage, remove external parasites, and clean and repair damaged feathers.

Despite the best care, feathers can become ragged and worn. Adult red-tails undergo a plumage molt each year whereby old, worn feathers are replaced by strong, new ones. The feathers are lost and replaced one by one or a few at a time in spring and summer months, so that the hawk is never rendered flightless or put at a great disadvantage during the molting process. The western red-tail at right shows off a bright new rectrix, or tail feather, growing in to replace one recently lost.

Head scratching is another behavior commonly observed in perched Red-tailed Hawks. The talons are used to uproot and evict external parasites, such as feather lice, from the top of the head, ear, and eye regions. A careless or overzealous bird can potentially do more damage to itself than to its pests.

A long bout of perching demands frequent stretching. This juvenile, caught in midstretch, is extending its right wing and leg at the same time while balancing on the left leg. The tail is also fanned to the right. Sometimes a stretching bird will lean forward and extend both wings for several seconds before resuming the original perching posture. This odd-looking spectacle may be mistaken by a casual observer for an aborted takeoff by an indecisive bird.

When a Red-tailed Hawk is not perched, it is usually soaring with the clouds, high above the earth. Watching a red-tail command the sky on fixed wings, seemingly without effort, can be inspirational. With its broad, slotted wings providing substantial surface area in relation to body mass, a red-tail is said to possess low wing loading. Such a bird is able to remain buoyant in the atmosphere with relatively little energy expenditure. The red-tail is much better adapted for sustained soaring flight than is the American Kestrel, seen here sharing a scrap of sky with its fellow raptor.

Rising columns of air, called thermals, provide a source of lift for soaring birds. Thermals are formed when the sun heats the earth unevenly, causing air above some areas to warm rapidly and begin to rise. A red-tail will typically "catch" a thermal and gain altitude by spiraling upward within it. The bird can economically cover long distances by climbing high in one thermal, then gliding down to catch another, and so on. Wind currents, deflected upward by landforms or other features of the landscape, also provide lift for soaring hawks. Thermals and deflected wind currents create important aerial highways for migrating raptors. Red-tailed Hawks use soaring for purposes of foraging, thermoregulation, courtship, territorial display, reconnaissance, and perhaps recreation, as well as migration.

A soaring red-tail sometimes attracts unwanted attention from crows or other birds. These smaller birds often gather in numbers to harass or "mob" a flying or perched raptor. Perhaps the goal is to discourage a potentially dangerous predator from hanging around the area. Mobbing may also serve to alert the neighborhood to the presence of a predator, reducing the chances of a sneak attack. Although there may be some safety in numbers, it doesn't pay for a mobbing bird to approach a raptor too closely. Twice I have seen a flying red-tail suddenly wheel in midair and strike a crow with its outstretched talons. On one of these occasions, several feathers exploded from the crow where the red-tail made contact. In both cases, the crows aborted their mobbing sortie without further incident.

Whereas some other North American buteos, such as the Red-shouldered, Ferruginous, and Swainson's hawks, have suffered marked reductions in distribution and abundance in certain geographic regions, the Red-tailed Hawk has slowly expanded its range over the last several decades. The chief reason is the red-tail's versatility. This bird exhibits amazingly broad tastes in diet, foraging and breeding habitat, and nesting substrates.

Red-tails may be found in evergreen and deciduous woodlands, plains and mountain grasslands, croplands, rangelands, shrub-steppe and desert scrub environments, urban parks, and even tropical rain forests. They occupy a wide range of elevation, from near the peaks of towering mountains to sea level. In addition to adequate prey populations, the critical factor that apparently makes an area attractive and habitable to a Red-tailed Hawk is the presence of some open patches interspersed with trees or other elevated perch and nest sites. Even where red-tails occupy tropical forests, as in Puerto Rico, they tend to hunt from above the canopy as if it were a patch of open pasture.

Human activities often create just the kind of mosaic of wooded, parkland environment that benefits red-tails, and human-built structures can provide excellent observation and hunting posts. This young bird, however, might do well to settle for a slightly less tenuous perch site in its urban jungle.

In some regions of the northern Great Plains, fire suppression by humans has allowed groves of aspen and other trees to invade what were formerly vast expanses of open grassland. The addition of trees to these areas has led to the decline of open-country obligates, such as the Ferruginous Hawk, and the expansion of parkland-loving species, such as the Red-tailed Hawk.

In some regions of the midwestern and southeastern United States, formerly unbroken tracts of bottomland forest have been partially cleared, creating a patchwork of open and wooded country. The occurrence of Red-shouldered Hawks has declined in these areas, while the occurrence of red-tails has increased.

2

Courtship and Incubation

Reproduction is a biological imperative for wild species, but not all individuals are equally successful at it. The genetic material of individuals that produce many offspring over their lifetimes is better represented in the population than is the genetic material of individuals that are less successful. Those genetically determined characteristics—both behavioral and physical—that help some individuals reproduce more successfully than others thus become more prevalent in the population.

To successfully reproduce, a hawk must find and attract a mate, select an appropriate nest site, build an adequate nest, defend a territory, produce and incubate viable eggs, and feed and nurture young until they are able to fend for themselves. Inappropriate behavior related to any of these activities can undermine reproductive success. Thus, the largely stereotypical behavior patterns associated with Red-tailed Hawk courtship and reproduction exist because they have proved successful for generations past.

For the Red-tailed Hawk, activities directly related to reproduction take up about half of each year. Red-tails are typically monogamous, and most pairs are thought to stay together for life. If one member of a pair dies, however, the surviving mate will form a new pair-bond in short order. There are a few scattered reports of two females being attended at a nest by one male, but these cases are anomalies.

Not all Red-tailed Hawks in a population are able to attract mates and breed in a given year. Most individuals do not breed until they are at least two years old and have attained the red tail indicative of adult plumage. Females are generally in shorter supply than males and stand a better chance than males of breeding in the first year.

The dramatic courtship displays of Red-tailed Hawks begin in late winter, often on overwintering grounds far from the nesting area. During courtship, both birds of a pair soar in great circles high above the ground. Frequently, they will climb beyond the sight of an observer on the ground. At some point, the male begins a series of spectacular dives in view of the female. Both birds may crisscross in front of each other and dangle their legs conspicuously during these aerial maneuvers. Eventually, the male zooms to a position just above the female and touches her with his legs extended. In the bottom photo, the smaller male is dropping down toward the female just prior to contact. Both birds may touch each other with bills or talons. When the two birds interlock talons, they often spiral at great speeds toward the ground. This talon-grappling spiral usually ends before the pair reaches the ground, but one report describes a pair that hit the ground, bounced about a foot, then disentangled and flew away. Neither bird showed any obvious sign of injury.

These breathtaking courtship acrobatics usually occur in bouts of five to ten minutes and may be accompanied by repeated, cacophonous vocalizations. The most common vocalization is the distinctive *kee-eeee-arrr* scream, which lasts about two to three seconds. This familiar call ascends for the first two seconds and falls rapidly at the end. Although it is usually associated with aerial maneuvers, it is also uttered by perched birds.

Another vocalization often heard during courtship is a short, shrill chirp. It may be uttered by one or both birds of a pair.

Courtship between Red-tailed Hawks wouldn't be complete without courtship feeding, whereby the male captures prey and offers it to his mate. Frequently, the offer is made during aerial displays. One windy April day some years ago in Colorado, I was enthralled by the acrobatics of a pair of courting red-tails high above me. The male disappeared for several minutes and suddenly reappeared above his mate with something long and ropelike dangling from his talons. The female rolled over, presented her talons in the classic talon-grappling fashion, and seized the object. Almost immediately, however, it fell from the female's grasp and plummeted to earth. Neither bird made any attempt to retrieve the fallen object, so I investigated. After searching the area for several minutes, I found a freshly killed, 2-foot-long Western rattlesnake.

The elaborate and sometimes dangerous courtship behavior of Red-tailed Hawks and other raptors presumably helps advertise general fitness and hunting ability. During incubation and brooding periods, the male bears primary responsibility for providing himself and his mate with food. A male that is unable to provide his mate with food during courtship would probably not be a good provider. Beyond its advertisement value, courtship feeding may provide the female with important resources she needs to produce eggs and initiate the nesting cycle. Although the emphasis is traditionally on the importance of the male conveying his fitness to the female during courtship, information is conveyed in both directions. The female is an active participant in aerial courtship displays, and her performance presumably provides fitness cues to the male.

Courtship is most frequent and intense early in the breeding season, prior to egg laying. But some elements of courtship behavior continue throughout the nesting period and can even occur well outside the breeding season. Presumably, these displays serve to reinforce the long-term pair-bond.

Red-tailed Hawks are intensely territorial
during the breeding season. Once the pair
arrives in the nesting area and selects a nest
site, the breeding territory is established
around the nest site by one or both members
of the pair. A territory is that portion of a red-
tail's home range that is actively defended.
It may function to provide the breeding pair
access to adequate resources for raising their
young. The size of the defended area may
vary greatly, depending on prey and perch
distribution, physical features of the landscape, and the number of potential competitors attempting to nest in the general area.
Territories are defended against other red-
tails but may also be defended against other
raptors, such as Swainson's Hawks. Red-tails
advertise territorial boundaries with flight
displays and vocalizations similar to those
exhibited during courtship. Intruders may
be chased or violently attacked with open
talons. Talon grappling may occur between
the territory holder and the intruder.

When perched, a red-tail may initially
meet an intruder with a distinctive aggressive
posture. The head and body are held erect;
feathers on the top of the head, neck, and
upper breast are raised; the bill is slightly
open; and the eyes are fixed on the interloper.

Selection of a nest site is a duty shared by
both members of a pair. After a pair has
nested together, they generally return to the
same area to nest in successive years. Red-

tails nest in a wide variety of habitats and situations, but some characteristics are common
to nearly all nest sites: unimpeded access to the nest from above and an elevated, expansive
view of the countryside below. The large nest in the crook of this towering conifer illustrates
the essential characteristics of red-tail nest sites. In wooded areas, the nest is usually placed
on a solid foundation, high in a tall tree. The nest tree is often near the edge of an opening,
but occasionally it may be located well within a large forest stand. If the local topography is
varied, nests are typically located in trees on elevated hills or ridges.

In appropriate habitat, a red-tail will exploit almost any elevated structure to support a nest. Tall, sturdy saguaro cacti provide adequate support for red-tail nests in the southwestern United States and Mexico. In one study conducted in Arizona, red-tails nested exclusively in saguaro. Where they are sympatric with saguaro-nesting Harris' Hawks, red-tails typically choose to nest in taller, more isolated saguaros.

Where available, cliff ledges are used for nesting. Ledges limit access for many potential nest predators, including humans, and usually provide the red-tail parents with a commanding view of a good portion of their territory. The location of such a nest is often given away by the excrement "whitewash" splattered on adjacent walls.

In urban environments, architectural niches on tall buildings may substitute nicely for irregular cliff faces. For several years, assorted red-tail pairs have delighted New York City birdwatchers by setting up housekeeping high on the facade of an exclusive apartment building on Fifth Avenue, near Central Park. For opportunistic Red-tailed Hawks, it seems that where there's a will, there's a way. Similar nest sites have been reported in Dallas and in Troy, New York. In other urban and human-altered environments, red-tails have been known to place nests on billboards, high-voltage transmission towers, and power poles.

Red-tails usually begin establishing their breeding territories and building their nests by early March, although timing varies with geographic region. Nest building has been reported as early as December in Arizona and as late as mid-April in Alberta, Canada. The nest itself is constructed of sticks and twigs, each of which is usually less than an inch in diameter. Green conifer sprigs are typically placed on the outside of the nest early in construction. It is speculated that the sprigs may function as a signal, perhaps to other hawks, that this nest is under construction. Alternatively, greenery placed outside and inside the nest may act as a pesticide, killing or discouraging insects or lice.

The entire nest is typically 25 to 30 inches (63 to 76 centimeters) in diameter. The inner bowl is usually about 5 to 6 inches (13 to 15 centimeters) deep and lined with strips of bark, fresh green twigs from conifer or deciduous trees, and other plant materials. Both members of the pair help with nest construction, but the female takes primary responsibility for shaping and lining the bowl.

Nesting material is carried to the nest site in the bill. This bird is about to contribute a fresh green sprig to nest construction. Most construction activities take place in the morning, and the hawks are very wary of human activity or other disturbance nearby. Close approach or repeated disturbance by humans may cause the birds to abandon nest-building activities. If uninterrupted, construction is usually completed in four to seven days.

The same nest may be used in successive years by the same pair. Red-tails usually return to the same nesting territory year after year. When a nest is reused, it is refurbished with sticks and fresh lining. Often a pair will build or refurbish two or more nests in the same area before finally settling on one. A nest may be left vacant for one or more years before being refurbished and used again. Nests constructed by Red-tailed Hawks may be occupied in future years by other birds. In the East, such opportunists include the Great Horned Owl, Barred Owl, American Crow, Red-shouldered Hawk, and Broad-winged Hawk. In the West, red-tail nests may be used by the Great Horned Owl, Swainson's Hawk, Ferruginous Hawk, and Common Raven, among others. Red-tails may also turn the tables and use nests built in previous years by Red-shouldered, Broad-winged, Ferruginous, and Swainson's hawks. Great Horned Owls typically nest much earlier than Red-tailed Hawks, and in some instances, red-tails use the nest occupied earlier the same year by Great Horned Owls. Where the nesting periods overlap, it is not uncommon for red-tails to nest in close proximity to a pair of Great Horned Owls occupying a nest built by the red-tails in a previous year. The neighborhood can become rowdy when these two species simultaneously occupy nests near each other. Sporadic bouts of aggression between the two species are separated by an uneasy truce. Aggression, occasionally including attacks with open talons, may be initiated and "won" by either species. Rarely are adults severely injured from these encounters, but chances for nesting success may be diminished due to added energy expenditure and stress.

Red-tail nests may be subleased by other tenants. On three separate occasions, in three different states (Arkansas, Oklahoma, and Colorado), I observed English Sparrows nesting in lower sections of Red-tailed Hawk nests while red-tails occupied the penthouse. In each case, both hawks and sparrows successfully raised young with no apparent interference from each other.

Other species, such as the Western Kingbird, shown here, frequently nest in the outer compartments of large raptor nests. Aside from Red-tailed Hawks, Golden Eagles, Ferruginous Hawks, and Swainson's Hawks are among the raptors that commonly host these opportunists. Such relationships may be of mutual benefit, whereby insect-eating songbirds control pests near the nest, and raptors chase away crows and other potential nest predators.

After a pair of Red-tailed Hawks selects a nest site and begins nest building or refurbishment, it may be up to five weeks before egg laying commences. In northern latitudes, where there is a relatively small window for optimal breeding conditions, the interval between nest site selection and egg laying may be as short as three weeks. The female may begin egg laying as early as mid-March (even earlier in Puerto Rico and other areas south of the U.S.) or as late as mid-May, depending on geographic region, local conditions, and individual variation.

Among raptors, larger species tend to produce fewer eggs than smaller species. For example, the Golden Eagle typically produces two eggs per nesting attempt, whereas the American Kestrel typically produces four to six eggs. The number of eggs laid per red-tail nest varies based on many factors, but in most cases, the average is two to three. Clutch sizes as small as one egg and as large as five eggs have been reported, however. Average clutch sizes tend to be larger in northwestern and smaller in southeastern portions of the species' range. However, the number of eggs laid may be adjusted to food availability in a given year and locale. More information from long-term studies is needed for biologists to understand the complex relationship between food availability and clutch size. A red-tail pair raises only one brood per year, but if the first clutch of eggs is destroyed, the female will lay a second and, rarely, a third replacement clutch, often in an alternative nest.

Red-tailed Hawk eggs are mostly white or off-white in color. They are dull, rather than shiny, and may be marked with irregular buffy, reddish, or brown specks and streaks. The eggs are about the size of chicken eggs, and each weighs roughly 6 percent of the female's body weight. An average clutch may therefore represent 12 to 18 percent of the female's body weight. Generally, the clutch weight of larger raptors represents a smaller proportion of body weight than the clutch weight of smaller raptors. For example, the average clutch weight of a Golden Eagle represents less than 10 percent of the female's body weight. In contrast, the average clutch weight of an American Kestrel represents more than 50 percent of the female's body weight.

Once egg laying commences, the female Red-tailed Hawk typically lays an egg every other day until the clutch is complete. The prospective parents begin incubating as soon as the first egg is laid. The female is responsible for most of the incubation, but the male takes over for a few hours during each twenty-four-hour period. As the eggs near hatching, the male spends less time incubating. The male provides most food for himself and his mate through the incubation period, but the female may also hunt for herself. If prey availability is low, the eggs may be left alone for up to thirty minutes while both parents are hunting. It is important that the eggs be kept warm as they develop. If both parents must leave the eggs frequently or for long periods, chances for successful development and hatching are reduced. For this reason, it is very important not to disturb nesting birds, especially during the critical incubation period.

It is often difficult to see an incubating parent on the nest. To warm and protect the eggs, the parent settles down deep in the bowl. Incubating females develop a temporary bare area, called a brood patch, among the feathers of the lower abdomen. This allows the female's bare skin, rich with blood vessels, to come into direct contact with the eggs and keep them near 100 degrees F (38 degrees C). Frequently, especially during the early incubation period, the female turns and rearranges the eggs with her bill to ensure even warming, prevent internal material from sticking to the inside of the shell, and perhaps equalize the influence of gravity on ovum and embryo development.

As development proceeds, the egg loses water (as water vapor) through the shell. Moderate water loss in this way creates an air-filled space in the blunt end of the egg, where the chick draws its first breath before breaking through the shell. By the time the chick is ready to break out, the eggshell is considerably thinner than it was when first laid. This is because calcium from the eggshell is incorporated into the skeleton of the developing chick.

Some chemicals, such as the pesticide DDT and its residues, interfere with a female's ability to incorporate enough calcium into eggshells. When shells are too thin, they may break immediately with the weight of the incubating female. Alternatively, thin-shelled eggs may allow too much water to escape, or simply not provide enough calcium for the chick to develop properly. The end result is a failed reproductive effort. Before DDT use was banned in the United States in 1972, several raptor species, including the Peregrine Falcon, Osprey, and Bald Eagle, suffered staggering reproductive losses and became threatened with extermination due to pesticide poisoning. These species were most susceptible to pesticide poisoning by virtue of their position at the end of long food chains. Raptors that feed on other birds or on aquatic prey are especially vulnerable to environmental poisons such as DDT.

With help from scientists, wildlife managers, and conservationists, the North American species threatened by the effects of DDT poisoning earlier in this century have largely rebounded. The threat has not completely disappeared, however, because pesticides like DDT leave toxic residues in the environment for many years. Many of these substances are still being used outside the United States. Neither Red-tailed Hawks nor other large buteos at the end of relatively short, terrestrial-based food chains have suffered large-scale reproductive losses from DDT.

3

Hatching and Fledging

The Red-tailed Hawk nesting cycle generally coincides with a period of high prey availability. Migratory birds have returned from overwintering grounds to the south; reptiles, amphibians, and ground squirrels have emerged from underground hibernacula; and insects abound. Reproduction is the order of the season for all these groups and others. That translates to an abundance of young, vulnerable birds and small mammals. If red-tails begin their reproductive activities on nature's schedule, they will be rewarded with plentiful and vulnerable prey at a time when they need it most—when their eggs hatch and their growing chicks begin demanding food.

40

Red-tailed Hawk parents typically incubate the eggs for at least twenty-eight days before the first one begins to hatch. The incubation period may be extended up to thirty-five days. As hatching nears, the chick begins calling softly from inside the egg. The mother answers the chick and remains on or very near the nest during this critical period. The chick begins chipping away at the inside of the eggshell with a small, hard bump on the tip of its bill. This "egg tooth" falls off shortly after helping the chick escape its confining shell. It often takes a red-tail chick a full day or more to open a small hole in the shell. After several more hours of work, the chick opens a hole large enough to break through to freedom.

When a Red-tailed Hawk chick first emerges from the egg, its eyes are open, and its body is covered with a layer of white down feathers. The feathers may be wet at first, but they soon dry to form a fluffy coat. The chick is helpless and completely dependent on its parents for protection and nourishment. The female must cover, or brood, young chicks continuously at first to protect the youngsters from excessive heat and cold, precipitation, and other environmental threats. The female continues to brood the chick daily for thirty to thirty-five days after the first chick's hatching. The male usually does not help brood the chicks. After the first few days of nearly continuous protection, the female spends progressively less time per day brooding. The actual time the female spends brooding varies with weather and many other factors but typically ranges from one to five hours per day through most of the brooding period. A newly hatched chick weighs only about 2 ounces (60 grams) and can do little more during the first several hours after hatching than weakly raise its head and open its bill to accept food from a parent. A Red-tailed Hawk chick, like all newly hatched raptor chicks, is an odd-looking beast, with legs and head quite large in proportion to the rest of its body.

Because incubation begins with the first egg laid, often well before the clutch is complete, hatching is usually spread over several days. This asynchronous hatching has profound implications for nestling survival and dynamics. Generally, the first chicks to hatch get a head start on growth and thus have an advantage over later chicks. When parents bring food to the nest, the siblings vie with one another for each morsel. If food is scarce, it is typically the older chicks that monopolize the nourishment and continue to grow larger, stronger, and more aggressive. The younger chicks grow progressively weaker and may die of starvation. This may sound cruel, but if food were equally divided among all chicks, they all might receive inadequate nourishment and die. By allowing the chicks to compete among themselves, the parents stand the best chance of producing the greatest number of healthy chicks possible under the existing environmental conditions. When there is enough food to go around, however, even the youngest chick in the nest gets a healthy portion.

Among larger raptors, especially eagles, the older, larger chick often kills its weaker sibling. An eagle chick requires an enormous amount of nourishment, and parents are rarely able to provide enough prey to adequately nourish two chicks. Why, then, do eagles typically expend the energy to lay two eggs? The second egg may provide insurance, in case the first is not viable or is destroyed. The second egg may also allow the parents to double their productivity if food is particularly abundant in a given year, although the elder chick often kills its sibling even when food is plentiful. This siblicide scenario is sometimes referred to as Cain and Abel syndrome, or "cainism." Although cainism may occur among Red-tailed Hawk and other buteo siblings, it is much less common than among eagles. It is virtually unknown in falcons and smaller hawks.

Red-tailed Hawk chicks, like the young of most raptors, grow very quickly. The rapid growth is facilitated by a high-protein diet. Energy gained from the diet can be directed toward growth and development, rather than thermoregulation, because the chicks are brooded by the mother. During the first five to seven days after hatching, chicks retain their soft white down and remain weak. They may bounce and shudder weakly in the nest and utter soft peeps. As the chicks grow older, the down turns a dingy medium gray and becomes a bit more coarse. Between about twelve and fifteen days after hatching, the chicks begin to peck and tear at food placed in the nest and utter high, whistling calls when the parents approach.

By two weeks post-hatching, the chicks sit erect most of each day. The down remains largely gray, but the upper legs and the top and back of the head sport white down. On or about day fifteen, the sheaths of the primary wing feathers appear. The young birds measure about 9 inches (23 centimeters) in length at this age.

When the young reach approximately seventeen to twenty days of age, the little wing tips are dark brown, though the down on the body remains gray. The chicks are aggressive and strike out at intruders with open talons. They also begin cautiously exploring the nest. The adventurer here is perhaps two to three days older than his or her more sedentary sibling. The older chick is approximately 10 inches (25 centimeters) in length.

By the time the young are twenty-five days old, the dark primary feathers contrast sharply with the gray body down and white head down. Some dark feathers have also appeared on the shoulder, along the side of the back. These are called scapular feathers or, simply, scapulars. The center chick in this brood illustrates this stage. These young birds can be quite aggressive toward intruders, though they are generally not efficient at closing talons and grasping objects with authority.

The three chicks shown here range from about four to five weeks post-hatching. The youngest chick, on the left, is about 13 inches (33 centimeters) long. The wing feathers and scapulars sport some dark brown, in marked contrast to most of the dorsum (back). There is also a dark patch of feathers beginning to cover the ear openings on either side of the head. The top of the head is still covered with white down, and there are other patches of white down overlying the base of the tail and the base of the wing feathers.

More than half of the white down on the head has been replaced by brown juvenile feathers on the chick on the right. The breast is almost completely feathered, and the dorsal part of the body is almost completely covered with dark feathers. Some patches of white or gray down are visible, giving the chick a disheveled appearance. At this stage, chicks may frequently be seen perching on the rim of the nest stretching their necks and wings.

The dorsal part of the wing is completely feathered and the chicks are essentially full grown by the time they reach thirty-nine to forty days of age. About 10 to 25 percent of the head may still be white in some birds, however. Before these well-fed chicks leave the nest, they will probably outweigh their parents.

The young birds may leave the nest with a decent chance of survival anytime after about thirty-nine days of age, but their chances of survival generally improve with more days in the nest. Almost all young are completely feathered and leave the nest by forty-two to forty-six days of age. Departure from the nest is commonly termed fledging, and it is a momentous point in any bird's life. It is the time when a young bird begins the critical transition from depending on parental care for food and protection to becoming completely self-reliant.

During the nestling period, between hatching and departure from the nest, the male does the majority of the hunting and delivers food to the nest. The specifics of delivery may vary greatly from pair to pair. While still in elementary school, I had the opportunity to observe two Red-tailed Hawk nests within about a half mile of each other near my hometown of Fort Smith, Arkansas. At one nest, the male regularly delivered fox squirrels, cottontails, woodrats, and other prey items to a large branch high in a tree next to the nest tree. The female waited for the male to depart, then flew out to secure the item and brought it back to the nest. Once back at the nest, she proceeded to tear the prey into small pieces for the young. Occasionally, she ate large portions of the prey item herself before carrying the remainder to the nest. At the other nest I watched, the female often met the male as he brought prey directly to the nest. At this nest, the male passed the food to the female and stood beside her as she tore the food into small pieces and presented it to the chicks.

The female may perform some hunting duties, especially late in the nestling period. At one nest I studied in Oklahoma, the male virtually disappeared the last week before the two young fledged. During that period, the female departed frequently during early to midmorning, and again in late afternoon, to secure food for the chicks. She stayed on or near the nest during the heat of the day, providing some shade for her young. Shortly after the young fledged, the male reappeared and helped attend the fledglings. I never discovered the reason for his week-long disappearance.

For the first four to five weeks after the chicks hatch, the female tears prey items into small pieces before offering them to her young. Later, the prey is rather unceremoniously dropped in the nest for the chicks to tear apart on their own. The frequency of food delivery and the amount of food delivered vary greatly, depending on prey availability, hunting ability of the parents, and the number of chicks in the nest. There is no evidence that the frequency of food delivery or the amount of food delivered varies with the age or size of the chicks.

Prey is usually delivered about ten to fifteen times a day, during daylight hours only. With each delivery, the parents keep a wary eye out for potential predators that could be alerted to the presence of the nest by the feeding activity. In various studies from different regions of the Red-tailed Hawk breeding range, researchers have reported a daily average of 8 to 18 ounces (219 to 520 grams) of food per chick provided by the parents. Near the end of the nestling period, prey remains tend to pile up in the nest, creating an unsightly and decidedly unsanitary nursery. Early in the nestling period, however, prey remains are usually removed from the nest within several hours of delivery.

Prey items brought to the young essentially reflect the adult diet, which reflects food available in the nesting habitat. These prey items were recovered from an urban nest in the eastern United States. The chicks were evidently fed a varied diet that included, among other things, gray squirrels and a pigeon bearing leg bands.

Ever versatile, the Red-tailed Hawk readily adapts to the local fare wherever it nests. A nest in an arid western site gave up the prey remains shown below. Snakes and cottontails consti-tuted at least a portion of the diet in this area.

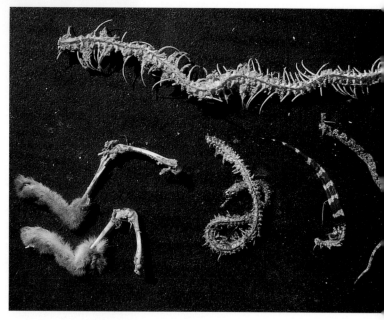

Three chicks from this saguaro nest have survived to nearly fledging age, but despite the best efforts of the parents, the nestling period is fraught with danger for the youngsters. Potential sources of mortality include exposure to weather, starvation, siblicide, predation, disease, parasitism (especially by blood-sucking flies in the genus *Eusimulium*), and even trampling by parents.

Great Horned Owls are among the most frequent predators of red-tail chicks. Eagles, too, prey on nestlings. On several occasions, live Red-tailed Hawk chicks have been found in Bald Eagle nests. In each case, the chick was far too young to fly. The most reasonable explanation was that one of the eagle parents had brought a red-tail chick to the nest as food but did not kill it immediately. The begging chick subsequently elicited feeding behavior from the eagle parents. In at least two such situations, Red-tailed Hawk chicks successfully fledged from Bald Eagle nests.

This family has weathered all the potential rigors of a bustling metropolitan environment to reach the point where two youngsters are about ready to leave the nest. In many areas, the most common source of nest failure is human interference. Repeated or severe disturbance by humans can cause red-tail parents to abandon eggs or nestlings altogether. Generally, the chances that the parents will abandon a nest decline as the nesting season progresses. Even when the parents do not completely abandon the young, excessive parental absence increases nestling exposure to weather and predation and may cause nestlings to become undernourished.

Red-tailed Hawk parents may keep a watchful eye out for danger but do not typically put up a vigorous defense when humans approach an active nest. A parent generally settles deeper down into the bowl of the nest to shrink from view or flies away immediately. Late in the nestling period, after substantial parental investment in the year's nesting attempt, parents tend to be a bit more aggressive toward human disturbance and less apt to abandon the nest. But even at this stage, the aggression usually consists of one or both parents soaring over the intruder or the nest, screaming their harsh disapproval of events below. This approach to defending the nest from human intruders is typical of most other buteos. It is in sharp contrast, however, to the vigorous defense exhibited by some other groups of raptors, especially the swift-flying hawks in the genus *Accipiter.* I was almost knocked from my horse by an attacking Northern Goshawk in Wyoming. My crime was approaching within about 30 yards of a nest previously unknown to me.

For a few days after leaving the nest, fledglings typically stay nearby. They often perch among branches of the nest tree, nagging parents for food. They may even return to the nest, especially after dark. Their initial attempts at flight are clumsy at best; crash landings are common.

After trying out its wings, this young bird performs an awkward balancing act on a dead branch. Whether a crash landing leads to mortality or is just a comedic learning experience depends largely on the environment surrounding the nest.

If they survive these initial attempts, fledglings rapidly improve and typically master flight within several days. This juvenile, only about two days out of the nest, seems to be getting the hang of being a full-fledged Red-tailed Hawk.

The full crop on this fledgling indicates a recent meal. It may be ready to attempt flight soon, but it will be weeks before it is capable of feeding itself entirely on its own. In the meantime, the parents will continue to provide food. Red-tail parents often present live prey to juveniles during this period, perhaps in an attempt to help the young birds learn to kill.

Initially, the siblings stay near one another. They may spend a good deal of time on the ground, pouncing on abundant insects or other small, relatively easily captured prey. These two sibling insect hunters show off their fresh juvenile plumage in the filtered rays of sunlight dancing through their woodland home.

"Prey" often consists of inanimate objects during this period, as recent fledglings learn to judge distance and seize objects securely with their formidable talons. This proud youngster has captured a stick. I have watched young red-tails play with sticks, corncobs, and many other objects during this stage in their development. They may seize an object, fly skyward with it, and then alternately drop and catch it in midair. No doubt this play behavior serves to hone a young predator's hunting skills.

As the recently fledged juvenile birds become more proficient hunters, the family wanders increasingly farther from the nesting area. During this period, the flying and hunting skills of the young are sharpened. Hunting methods of the youngsters develop gradually. For the first two to three weeks after leaving the nest, juveniles hunt mostly insects and other invertebrate prey. These hunting forays are limited to short, direct flights between elevated perches and the ground. By four to six weeks after leaving the nest, juveniles usually begin chasing vertebrate prey. The rate of success is typically very low, as the young birds learn to distinguish between appropriate and inappropriate targets. They may spend a great deal of valuable energy pursuing inappropriate "prey," including coyotes, foxes, badgers, and flocks of small passerines. Parents usually continue to supply vertebrate prey to their offspring during this period.

Juveniles may gradually broaden their range of hunting methods and increase their skills by learning from their parents or other Red-tailed Hawks. As the young birds gain experience, they incorporate more aerial searching techniques into their repertoire. At six to seven weeks past fledging, juveniles are usually adept at capturing small vertebrate prey. The parents may continue to provide some food at this point, but eventually they cease support, and the family dissolves. In some cases, the parents actively chase their young away. Essentially the same scenario occurs in most raptor species, but the juveniles' length of dependency on the parents varies greatly. Red-tail youngsters may depend on their parents for at least some food for more than two months after leaving the nest. When they finally become independent, juveniles embark on exploratory wanderings away from the breeding area. This large-scale movement is broadly termed dispersal.

4

Migration and Winter Range

As the breeding season comes to a close, recently fledged hawks begin fending for themselves and exploring more of their new world. The onset of fall brings the promise of winter and, for much of North America, heralds changes that profoundly impact the lives of Red-tailed Hawks. With each passing day, the amount of daylight available for hunting decreases. Much of the vegetation in some regions becomes dormant, and the abundance and activity of many herbivorous prey species decline.

Ground squirrels in western North America begin a long period of hibernation. Gone are the swarms of young ground squirrels that were such easy prey for hawks only a few months before. Other rodent species also essentially vanish during the frigid weather for prolonged periods of inactivity underground. When snow covers the ground and provides a protective blanket for small mammals, even active and plentiful rodents are difficult for hawks to hunt. Grasshoppers, crickets, and other insects, so plentiful in the warm, open fields of late summer, virtually disappear with the first frosty breaths of the new season. With their menu dwindling, many insect eaters also begin to vanish. Reptiles and amphibians seek refuge underground, where they will spend the winter fasting in hibernation. Many songbirds relocate southward to warmer climes and more plentiful food. With falling leaves, dropping temperatures, and declining prey, Red-tailed Hawks, too, must be prepared to migrate.

Migration is an important event in the natural history of many raptor species. It is an annual journey and relocation of individuals between different breeding and nonbreeding areas. The areas may be separated by a few dozen or a few thousand miles; they may resemble each other closely or be quite disparate. The unique migration pattern of each species has evolved because it improves access to resources required by that species in each season.

Some raptors entirely vacate their breeding range to occupy a separate range during the bulk of the nonbreeding season. For example, virtually all Swainson's Hawks vacate their breeding range in the grasslands and shrublands of western North America each year to spend the nonbreeding season in the grasslands of Argentina. Such a species is termed a complete migrant. Other species, including the Red-tailed Hawk, are known as partial migrants, because only some members of the species vacate their breeding range. The migration pattern exhibited by the Red-tailed Hawk is especially complex and may be heavily influenced by weather in a given year. The overall geographic range of the species stays virtually the same year-round, but most birds breeding in extreme northern latitudes move to more southerly latitudes for the winter. As a result, red-tails are more abundant in many central and southern regions during winter than during the summer months. Year-round residents in these regions are joined in winter by seasonal visitors from the north.

Across most of the species' range, juveniles are the first birds to begin southerly migration in the fall. The opposite is apparently true, however, among red-tails breeding in Alaska. Southerly movements may begin as early as August. Many factors combine to trigger the onset of fall migration. Decreasing photoperiod creates a restlessness in migratory birds, preparing them for the journey ahead. A local decline in prey availability may also contribute to the urge to migrate. The trigger for the beginning of the fall migratory journey may be a sharp decrease in barometric pressure, followed by a major drop in ambient temperature. These are factors usually associated with the passage of a cold front in early fall. Moderate to brisk winds from the north may also help trigger and enhance fall migration.

In all populations, adults tend to migrate the shortest distances from the breeding grounds, and they return to the breeding grounds earlier in the spring than do subadult birds. In some raptor species, females tend to migrate earlier in fall than males. Because it is generally not possible to determine the gender of free-flying Red-tailed Hawks, it is unknown for certain whether the timing of migration consistently differs between males and females.

Those red-tails breeding in northern latitudes in the eastern United States and Canada generally begin moving south in late August or early September. The latest migrants may not settle in their overwintering grounds until December. Hawk migration in eastern North America follows predictable pathways dictated by major topographic features. Thermals and wind currents deflected upward by major landforms are critical to migrating hawks. These uplifting currents of air allow large birds to cover great distances while expending far less energy than would otherwise be possible. Thermals do not readily form over large bodies of water, so most migrating hawks avoid oceans and large lakes. South-oriented peninsulas, such as Cape May, New Jersey, and Cape Charles, Virginia, along the east coast of the United States, act as funnels for migrating Red-tailed Hawks and other raptors. Regular raptor migration count stations have been established at such sites. Red-tailed Hawk fall migration has been well documented at Cape May for many years. An average of more than 1,600 red-tails is counted passing over this peninsula each fall. Roughly 75 percent of the birds are counted at Cape May between mid-October and mid-November, and peak numbers usually pass through in the first week of November.

One of the best-known raptor migration count stations in the world is Hawk Mountain, in southeastern Pennsylvania. This site is located on Kittatinny Ridge, one of many high ridges making up the continuous backbone of the Appalachians in the eastern United States. Migrating hawks use the thermal and deflected wind currents found along this mountain range to facilitate their journey.

Hawk Mountain has played a historical role in educating citizens about raptors and raptor conservation. Early in the twentieth century, local residents climbed Hawk Mountain to shoot migrating raptors for sport. Reports of the annual slaughter led conservationists to procure land at the site and establish a sanctuary. In 1934, Rosalie Edge, acting on behalf of the Emergency Conservation Committee, hired Maurice and Irma Broun as wardens of the sanctuary. Since that year, hundreds of observers have climbed to the site each fall to observe and count migrating raptors rather than shoot them.

Today, Hawk Mountain Sanctuary employs a year-round staff of professional educators and researchers, working to understand and interpret migrating raptors and other wildlife in the region. Each fall, well over 20,000 raptors, including 3,000 Red-tailed Hawks, are recorded migrating past Hawk Mountain. Migrating hawks often fly low along the ridge, providing observers with nearly a bird's-eye view. As at Cape May, peak numbers of red-tails are usually observed passing by Hawk Mountain in the first week of November.

Fall migration tends to begin and end earlier in western red-tail populations, but the timing is variable and may be influenced by local weather conditions and food availability. There are few concentrating points for migrating raptors in the western United States. Migration generally occurs across a broad front along the Pacific coast and across the Great Basin and Great Plains. The Rocky Mountains provide a leading line for migration, but few locations report large numbers of migrating hawks. One of the more consistent fall count sites in the western interior of North America is the Goshute Mountains lookout in Nevada. More than 2,000 fall-migrating red-tails are counted there in most years.

Some buteos tend to migrate in large flocks, called kettles. Swainson's Hawks and Broad-winged Hawks, especially, are notorious for this habit. In contrast, Red-tailed Hawks usually migrate singly or in small groups. During migration, red-tails may fly at air speeds exceeding 37 miles (60 kilometers) per hour and reach altitudes well over 2,800 feet (850 meters).

A peculiar feature of the migration pattern of many raptor species is a conspicuous lull in migratory activity reported during the middle of the day. This so-called noon lull is commonly noted at migration lookout stations across North America. It may last for two hours or more. Migratory flights on days with dense cloud cover are usually not punctuated by a noon lull. Several raptor species, including the Red-tailed Hawk, are reported to exhibit a pronounced noon lull. The most satisfactory explanation is that thermal currents are generally strongest during midday, and red-tails and other raptors use these currents to gain high altitudes, beyond the vision of observers on the ground.

The journey of migration is fraught with danger for its participants. Older birds presumably travel through areas they have not encountered for nearly a year. Juveniles encounter entirely unfamiliar areas with hazards unknown to them. It remains unclear just how migrating hawks decide where to go during migration and how to get there. Essentially, each bird must have some manner of internal map, relating its current position to where it wants to go, and an internal compass to keep the bird on course. Once a bird has completed a migratory journey, it may be able to use major landmarks to help it navigate the route again. But juvenile birds have no previous experience with landmarks. There may be an innate tendency to follow major topographic features, such as coastlines and mountain ranges, but that still leaves much unexplained about the process of navigation.

Red-tailed Hawks, along with other diurnal raptors, migrate almost exclusively during daylight hours. Experiments have shown that at least some daytime migrants are able to use the sun for orientation. Similarly, some bird species are known to have the ability to detect the earth's magnetic field and use it for orientation. Other cues possibly used by raptors to help them navigate during long-distance migration include wind direction, barometric pressure, ultraviolet light, and even low-frequency sounds caused by winds blowing across mountain ranges or other topographic features. Ongoing research into the relative importance of these and other factors to navigation should bring us closer to solving one of the great mysteries of bird migration.

The largest concentrations of overwintering Red-tailed Hawks usually occur in southern Iowa, northern Missouri, eastern Oklahoma, and California. High numbers of Harlan's red-tails tend to spend the winter in a broad band through eastern Kansas, eastern and central Oklahoma, central Missouri, and northeastern Arkansas. This adult Harlan's hawk takes advantage of an abandoned plow to inspect a patch of midwestern farm country.

Unfortunately, there is little information available to determine precisely how red-tails from other regional populations are distributed in the winter. The best indication comes from band recoveries. Researchers often capture adult and nestling raptors and place metal bands on their legs to help with population and behavioral studies. The Bird Banding Laboratory in Laurel, Maryland, administered by the Biological Resources Division of the United States Geological Survey, issues permits and provides materials to qualified bird-banders in the United States and maintains the national database of banding records. Recoveries of bands from deceased or live-captured birds can provide important information regarding seasonal movements, annual survivorship, and other population characteristics. In general, Red-tailed Hawk band recoveries indicate that migratory birds spend the winter in areas trending southeast of their breeding grounds.

Those hawks that survive the rigors of the migratory journey and arrive in suitable overwintering habitat face new challenges. Newly arrived migrants must assess hunting conditions and jockey for prime hunting areas with other migrants and year-round residents. Some red-tails return to the same area each winter, but not enough information exists to determine how widespread this phenomenon is within the species. Familiarity with the overwintering area would seem beneficial in finding food and avoiding danger.

Weather conditions can provide significant challenges to Red-tailed Hawks in winter. The energy demands for self-maintenance increase in cold weather, just as low temperatures, snow cover, and shorter periods of daylight make finding food more difficult. These factors help explain why most red-tails vacate areas in the extreme northern portions of the breeding range during winter.

Warm-blooded animals expend more energy just maintaining their body temperature in cold weather. Small, warm-blooded animals generally lose body heat to a cold environment faster than do larger ones. Nonetheless, even large hawks like the red-tail must keep as warm as possible and keep their internal furnaces supplied with plenty of food during cold weather. To reduce the amount of heat loss in cold weather, a perched red-tail will partially erect the contour feathers covering its body, thus trapping a layer of warm air next to the body. The feathers remain overlapped to provide a good insulative barrier. This technique gives the bird a bloated, fluffy look, exaggerating its already stocky appearance.

Significant heat may still be lost through the bare legs and feet. To reduce this loss, a red-tail usually perches on only one leg at a time, drawing the other up under the plumage covering the lower abdomen and upper leg. The position of the two legs may be alternated frequently.

Red-tails tend to squeeze every possible minute of hunting time into each short winter day. I have often observed red-tails leave their nighttime roost at the first sliver of daylight on a cold winter morning and not return to the roost until the last glimmer of light is fading from the horizon. Because they are not tied to a nest site or territory in winter, red-tails are free to abandon nonproductive hunting areas for more productive sites. As a result, the local concentration of red-tails in winter may fluctuate widely with food availability. Snow cover is one important factor that may reduce the availability of prey to hawks, and red-tails tend to avoid areas that are covered by snow for extended periods.

The winter habitat occupied by Red-tailed Hawks resembles the habitat they choose during summer months. In both seasons, they typically choose open areas with scattered trees or other elevated perches. Areas with rich, readily available food sources may attract high densities of Red-tailed Hawks. Fresh carrion is frequently exploited by buteos and eagles during winter, and it is not unusual to find several of these raptors, including Red-tailed Hawks, around a freshly killed deer, livestock, or other carcass.

Protected roost sites are critical to overwintering Red-tailed Hawks. On cold, windy nights, they tend to roost near the trunks of trees with dense branches or foliage. Conifers are frequently chosen in some areas. Although red-tails do not usually participate in the large, communal winter roosts typical of Bald Eagles, I have frequently found four to six red-tails roosting together in a small cluster of trees. During one winter at the Rocky Mountain Arsenal National Wildlife Refuge near Denver, Colorado, my graduate students and I often found Red-tailed Hawks roosting together with several Ferruginous Hawks in a grove of cottonwood trees. Only a few hundred yards away, in another cottonwood stand, was a large communal roost of Bald Eagles.

As winter loosens its grip on the landscape, giving way to bright skies and rising temperatures, migratory red-tails must soon abandon their overwintering grounds and begin the trek northward. If they return too early, they may find their breeding grounds still gripped by winter, with little prey available. If they return too late, all adequate nest sites may be taken, or they may miss the optimal window in which to successfully raise a family before autumn approaches once again. Generally, the factors that trigger spring migration are the opposite of those that trigger fall migration. Lengthening photoperiod, the passage of warm fronts, and warm southerly winds combine to induce red-tails to return to their breeding grounds. Spring migration may begin as early as February, but a few birds may not arrive on the breeding grounds until May or June.

Due to prevailing winds and other environmental conditions, spring migration routes may vary somewhat from those used in fall. Among spring migration count sites in eastern North America, Derby Hill Bird Observatory and Braddock Bay Raptor Research site in New York record relatively large numbers of Red-tailed Hawks. Derby Hill records more than 7,000 red-tails each spring. In the central region of the continent, Whitefish Point, Michigan, records nearly 2,000 red-tails during spring migration counts. In the Rocky Mountain West, the Dinosaur Ridge Raptor Migration Station near Denver averages nearly 1,000 red-tails each spring, with the peak flight occurring in early to mid-April.

5

Hunting and Diet

Above all else, the Red-tailed Hawk is a predator. It is armed with the tools, instincts, and skills of a predator. Many people are awestruck by the predatory prowess of a raptor, but some are repulsed and may even feel loathing or fear toward the successful hunter. To witness a red-tail initiate an all-out attack on its intended prey is akin to watching Deion Sanders flash toward an intended interception or Mary Lou Retton launch a perfect vault. Each is calling on exceptional physical skills honed through a lifetime to attempt a feat against heavy odds. The difference, of course, is that the very life of the hawk depends on its success.

When I first saw a Red-tailed Hawk exhibit its awesome hunting skills, I was perhaps eight years old. My father and I were out for an afternoon drive in hopes of spotting a gray fox, a few white-tailed deer, or other wildlife known to inhabit the sprawling military reservation where my dad was stationed. It was late October, and the sun was sinking fast in front of us. We were idling along at perhaps 30 miles an hour when my father pointed out a rabbit sitting in the open about 50 yards ahead and 20 yards off the left side of the road. The last rays of the sinking sun made the cottontail's ears glow like two golden miniature lightbulbs. Suddenly, a large brownish blur crossed our path from right to left. It was about 12 feet off the ground, dropping steadily. I vividly remember the blur taking on the form of a large hawk with eyes fixed forward. Just before it reached the rabbit, the hawk braked with wings and tail and thrust both legs forward. Dust flew, highlighted by streaks of sunlight, as the hawk's talons hit the rabbit, and both tumbled. I was absolutely spellbound as the hawk recovered quickly and deftly pounced on the tousled cottontail. We stopped the car, and I slowly rolled down my

window to get a better look. (A pair of binoculars was quickly added to that year's Christmas wish list.) The raptor had its back to us, its wings spread around the prize. It looked over its shoulder as if to say, "Back off. This is my dinner." For the first time, I saw the red, fan-shaped tail that later helped me identify the hawk from an illustration in my field guide. This was my first real introduction to the drama of predator-prey relationships, and it inspired me to explore further—something I've been doing now for more than thirty years. Each time I am fortunate enough to witness an episode like that one, I am filled with the same emotions I felt on that cool October afternoon: admiration for the skills displayed by the predator, sadness for the suffering experienced by the prey, and profound veneration for the daily adventure of life and death in nature.

The drama I witnessed with my father so many years ago is illustrative of the hunting tactics employed by the Red-tailed Hawk. Like most buteos, the red-tail is largely a sit-and-wait hunter that may perch patiently for hours scanning a favorite field or pasture for prey. Thanks to superb eyesight, a hawk on an elevated perch can effectively scrutinize a large area. Once prey is spotted, the red-tail sometimes leans forward and voids the digestive tract just before launching an attack.

The attack usually begins with a stiff-winged, silent glide directly down toward the target. This hunter appears to have begun its deadly descent on an intended victim below. If necessary, the hawk will shift into chase mode, with wings flapping.

If the chase lasts more than a few seconds, however, the prey stands a good chance of escaping. The great, broad wings of the red-tail are not well designed for the abrupt maneuvers necessary to pursue highly nimble flying or running prey.

When local weather conditions are conducive to soaring (moderate winds or strong thermals), Red-tailed Hawks may hunt from high above the ground. When prey is spotted from above, the hawk folds or sets its wings to drop (stoop) quickly from the sky and fall on its unsuspecting victim. Some published accounts indicate that this is the most common hunting technique employed by the Red-tailed Hawk. In my experience, however, far more attacks are launched from a perch than from the air. This helps explain why red-tail distribution is tied to the presence of elevated perch sites. Soaring flight is probably used most often by red-tails to assess prey activity across a large expanse of the home range, helping a hawk decide where to perch for the best chance of a successful hunt.

Some raptors, such as the American Kestrel, often hunt while hovering in one place above the ground. To accomplish this, they face into a brisk wind and stay aloft with shallow, rapid wing strokes. When prey is spotted, the hunter folds its wings to launch an attack. The Rough-legged Hawk, a close relative of the red-tail, uses this technique frequently, but I have observed it performed only occasionally by red-tails.

Under appropriate conditions, Red-tailed Hawks, especially juveniles such as the one at left, hunt on the ground, chasing down abundant grasshoppers or other insects.

Red-tails can be remarkably adaptable. In 1993, while studying the winter ecology of Ferruginous Hawks around a Colorado prairie dog colony, I found that these large buteos frequently hunted prairie dogs by standing on the ground behind a pile of dirt at a burrow entrance. When an unwary prairie dog emerged too far from its burrow, it was summarily ambushed by the hawk.

There were several Red-tailed Hawks in the area, and I often observed them characteristically perched on trees or utility poles overlooking the prairie dog colony. Vigilant prairie dogs easily spotted and avoided hawks perched conspicuously above them. At least one red-tail, however, took up the hunting technique of the Ferruginous Hawks. That bird, easily recognized by its unusually dark, reddish breast plumage, habitually perched on the ground near a prairie dog burrow. I never witnessed a successful attack, but I did see this bird feeding on prairie dogs on two separate occasions.

Many raptors pirate prey away from one another. Bald Eagles, for example, regularly steal fish from Ospreys and even prairie dogs from Ferruginous Hawks. Red-tails, too, can become pirates. The most frequently cited victims of red-tail piracy are Rough-legged Hawks and Northern Harriers. Sometimes a red-tail will harass another hawk in midair until it drops its freshly caught prey. The pirate may then deftly capture its stolen prize while still in the air or pounce on it when it hits the ground. A red-tail will also challenge another raptor on the ground for its meal.

I have witnessed two such instances. In one case, an adult Red-tailed Hawk successfully separated an adult male Northern Harrier from his freshly caught Red-winged Blackbird. In the other, absolutely remarkable, instance, an adult red-tail successfully drove two adult Ferruginous Hawks—both larger than the red-tail—away from a freshly killed prairie dog. I came upon the winter scene soon after one of the Ferruginous Hawks had made the kill. The second Ferruginous Hawk appeared and began challenging the first hawk for the prairie dog. Perhaps attracted by the melee, the red-tail landed on the ground a few yards away, watched the action for a few minutes, and then suddenly began attacking one of the Ferruginous Hawks. The red-tail repeatedly launched itself, talons first, at the Ferruginous Hawk until the latter flew away. The other Ferruginous Hawk stayed nearby on the ground and watched from a distance as the red-tail consumed nearly all of the prairie dog. Despite the feat of this particularly aggressive bird, red-tails are frequently victims of piracy. Golden Eagles, Bald Eagles, Ferruginous Hawks, and Rough-legged Hawks are among the raptor species that may rob red-tails.

Red-tails do not hunt randomly throughout the home range. Not surprisingly, they tend to spend a disproportionate amount of time in areas of the home range where they reap the greatest food reward for their hunting effort. The most rewarding hunting area is not necessarily that with the greatest prey abundance, however. If ground cover is too tall or dense, red-tails may have difficulty locating or capturing prey, no matter how abundant. Vegetation like this makes hunting very difficult.

If there are no perch sites available, red-tails may not be able to effectively ambush prey. Indeed, otherwise suitable hunting habitat is often avoided by Red-tailed Hawks if there are no elevated perch sites available. Ideal hunting habitat for red-tails includes moderate to high prey abundance, short or sparse ground cover, and plentiful elevated perch sites.

A red-tail uses its powerful talons, rather than its sharp bill, to initiate its attack on a potential prey animal. Typically, the hawk thrusts its open feet toward the prey and makes contact with one foot slightly in front of the other. The talons immediately seize the prey in a viselike grip. If the initial seizure does not incapacitate the prey, or if it is not quickly followed by a killing bite from the razor-sharp bill, the hawk can be injured by the struggles of its victim. A translucent eye covering, the nictitating membrane, closes completely over the hawk's eye from front to back at the instant of attack. This covering, visible here in a bird shortly after a kill, offers some protection from the scratches of struggling prey. The nictitating membrane is sometimes referred to as a third eyelid because it operates separately from the upper and lower eyelids that close to meet across the middle of the eye.

Despite all efforts and protective measures, birds of prey often bear scars on their legs, feet, and head from being bitten or scratched by prey animals. This hawk is trying to subdue a large and potentially troublesome Norway rat.

The bite can have more serious consequences if the prey is a poisonous snake. When attacking a snake, a red-tail typically snatches the animal in the middle of the body and kills it quickly with a bite to the head. Most snakes preyed upon by red-tails are nonpoisonous, but rattlesnakes show up regularly in the diet of some red-tail populations. In these encounters, careless hawks can become dead hawks.

When an attack is successful and the prey is secured, the hawk usually begins feeding immediately. Characteristically, the successful hunter fans its tail, spreads its wings, and hunkers over the prey. With this posture, the bird is said to be mantling its prey. The mantling posture, exhibited here by this juvenile red-tail, is an attempt to shield the prey from a would-be thief. Rabbit- or pheasant-sized prey is usually plucked and eaten at the site of the kill. Smaller items, or the remains of larger prey, may be brought to a perch for feeding. Occasionally, large carcasses are abandoned before feeding is complete. In winter, when temperatures hover around freezing, a red-tail may revisit a large carcass to feed for several days. In most cases, raptors leave very little of their prey behind to testify to the drama of the hunt.

After a meal, a red-tail usually cleans its bill meticulously. To accomplish this, the hawk rubs both sides of the bill against a tree branch, fence post, or similar structure.

Like most raptors, the Red-tailed Hawk is an opportunistic hunter. Owing to the broad geographic range of the species, its moderate size, and its opportunistic nature, the red-tail eats a wide variety of prey. Diet may vary considerably among seasons, geographic regions, and individuals. In general, most adults tend to prefer larger prey, up to the size of jackrabbits, when available. Young birds tend to include more small prey in their diets, even when larger prey is readily available. Most of our knowledge about raptor diets comes from examining prey remains from the nest site or regurgitated pellets of undigested fur, feathers, and bones. In wild birds, a pellet, or casting, usually includes undigested remains of several prey items ingested over a period of one to several days. Scientists collect pellets from underneath favored perches to determine hawk diets. In the laboratory, the pellets are carefully teased apart, and the fur, feathers, and skull and other bone fragments are identified with the aid of a microscope and museum reference collections. Common mammalian prey of the Red-tailed Hawk includes voles, deer mice, house mice, cotton rats, rice rats, pocket gophers, cottontails, snowshoe hares, jackrabbits, muskrats, ground squirrels, and tree squirrels.

According to some reports, tree squirrels are sometimes captured by two hawks working in tandem, whereby one hawk chases the squirrel around a tree and another hawk makes the grab. I have never witnessed this sort of team hunting, but it seems to fall short of the highly organized, cooperative hunts of Harris' Hawks. Members of a Harris' Hawk hunting team share food at the end of a successful hunt; there is no indication that red-tails do so. This Red-tailed Hawk certainly gives no indication of sharing its gray squirrel.

In some regions, birds make up a large proportion of the Red-tailed Hawk diet. Pheasant, quail, and waterfowl are common prey where they are readily available, but a wide variety of other species are also taken. There are few reports, however, of a red-tail capturing a bird in flight. Most avian prey is probably ambushed while perched on the ground or on a conspicuous singing post. Nesting birds make particularly vulnerable targets. Ever the opportunist, this red-tail plunders a robin's nest to feed its own young.

Reptiles and amphibians are regularly eaten by red-tails. In some circumstances, snakes may constitute more than 50 percent of the biomass eaten. Bull snakes, rat snakes, and garter snakes appear most often in the diet. Rattlesnakes and other poisonous snakes are also eaten, but they are included less frequently than would be expected from their abundance in the environment. This may indicate that red-tails tend to avoid poisonous snakes or that the activity patterns of these reptiles make them somehow less available to red-tails.

Where they are abundant, insects and other invertebrates may contribute significantly to the diet. Large crickets and grasshoppers are usually plentiful in grasslands and agricultural areas for a few weeks in late summer and early fall, and red-tails readily take advantage of this cornucopia. I once watched two juvenile and two adult red-tails hop around a large field for more than two hours, catching and eating grasshoppers. The scene often turned comical as the juveniles bounded awkwardly into each other in their pursuit of the same insect. Swainson's Hawks, close relatives of the red-tail, regularly gather by the hundreds to feed on crickets and grasshoppers just prior to fall migration. One warm September afternoon, I counted three Red-tailed Hawks, five Northern Harriers, and more than 800 Swainson's Hawks gorging themselves on insects in a newly hayed field in eastern Colorado. Raptors typically ingest food rapidly—more quickly than the avian stomach can handle. An expandable portion of the esophagus, called the crop, functions to store and soften food before it proceeds along the digestive tract. The distended crop on this bird attests to a recent hearty meal.

Besides insects, other invertebrates that frequently appear in the diet of red-tails include spiders, centipedes, crayfish, and earthworms. This last item is often taken in large numbers from the ground surface after a heavy rainfall. On Soccoro Island, west of the Baja peninsula, red-tails feed largely on land crabs.

Near caves where large numbers of bats enter and leave daytime roosts, local red-tails learn to capitalize on this abundant, if transient, food source. Despite their stocky, broad-winged form, some red-tails become quite adept at capturing bats in midair. The hawks sometimes slice through the middle of a dense stream of bats, reach out with open talons to seize a victim, and speed away. Alternatively, they may fly parallel with the stream and suddenly veer into it to grab a single bat.

Biologists are sometimes shocked to find hair from deer, elk, sheep, cattle, and other large mammals in Red-tailed Hawk pellets. The explanation, of course, is that red-tails feed on fresh carrion when it is available. Traffic deaths are a particularly important source of nutrition for red-tails in some areas, especially in winter. Another abundant source of carrion may be found near large poultry operations. Poultry workers sometimes discard carcasses of chickens or turkeys in large piles or spread them with manure in agricultural fields. When observed feeding on one of these carcasses, a Red-tailed Hawk may be wrongfully accused of killing poultry. No doubt red-tails occasionally prey on domestic poultry, but this species does not deserve the moniker "chicken hawk," as it is known in some rural regions of North America.

The amount of food a Red-tailed Hawk needs to sustain itself varies with many factors, including age, gender, ambient temperature, and activity patterns. In fall and winter months, a red-tail generally consumes an average of 4 to 5 ounces (130 to 150 grams) of food per day. That is the equivalent of about six to eight deer mice per day or one cottontail every four to six days. The small bird that has fallen victim to this hawk represents about half of a red-tail's average daily consumption during the nonbreeding season. During spring and summer, average daily food intake for adults may be only 3 to 4 ounces (80 to 90 grams), with females consuming slightly more than males. Weight loss for both males and females is often considerable during the busy breeding season.

Many of the prey items included in the diet of the Red-tailed Hawk are also prominent in the diets of other, coexisting raptor species. One of the most widely accepted principles of ecological theory, most commonly cited as the "competitive exclusion principle," holds that two species cannot coexist in the same place and time if they are too similar in their resource requirements. Unfortunately, ecological science may never progress sufficiently for us to be able to predict exactly how similar is too similar in all cases. There are simply too many variables that must be accounted for. Nonetheless, the competitive exclusion principle has encouraged natural scientists to closely examine similarities and differences in ecology among closely related species. When foraging behavior and diet have been compared between red-tails and other buteos occupying a common area, clear differences have emerged. The specifics vary with each situation, but in general, severe competition between red-tails and other raptors is avoided due to differences in prey selection, habitat use, and/or hunting method. For example, where Ferruginous Hawks and Red-tailed Hawks coexist, Ferruginous Hawks tend to hunt in more open areas, often without elevated perches nearby. Although both species may prey on rabbits, hares, and ground squirrels in a particular area, the more versatile red-tails generally include more birds, mice, voles, and other small mammals in their diets.

In the eastern United States, Red-tailed Hawks and Red-shouldered Hawks often share home ranges in broken woodland. There, red-tails tend to hunt in more open areas bordering the woodland, whereas red-shoulders tend to focus more on the wooded, riparian areas. Both species may include mice in their diets, but red-shoulders eat far more aquatic prey, such as frogs and crayfish, and red-tails are more apt to take larger mammals, such as squirrels. In each of these examples, severe competition between red-tails and other buteos is avoided due to differences in foraging habitat and the specific prey taken.

Red-tailed Hawks and Great Horned Owls are similar in size, feed largely on birds and mammals, and often share the same foraging habitat. Both species are widely distributed throughout North America and are considered generalist predators. Consequently, these two birds are sometimes assumed to overlap greatly in diet, representing daytime-nighttime versions of essentially the same predator. In fact, the diets of red-tails and Great Horned Owls that share the same hunting grounds overlap to some extent, but they generally take a different assortment of prey species.

6

Population Biology and Conservation

Because of their physical characteristics, lifestyles, and reproductive biology, birds of prey, as a group, are especially vulnerable to environmental changes caused by human activities. In general, raptors are large, long-lived predators that occur in low densities and reproduce at a relatively slow rate. Many have very specific habitat requirements and are dependent on the productivity of each of many separate links in the food chain below them. Depending on their specific prey, many raptors are highly vulnerable to pesticides and other environmental toxins. Historically, Red-tailed Hawks and other birds of prey have been directly persecuted as competitors with humans for game species and as threats to poultry and other livestock. Although direct persecution is no longer a widespread threat to birds of prey in the United States, it continues to threaten populations in other parts of the world.

In part because of their vulnerability to environmental change, and in part due to their charismatic appeal to many people, raptors have figured prominently in the worldwide conservation movement during the past several decades. The Bald Eagle and Peregrine Falcon have, in essence, served as poster models for the United States Endangered Species Act. Moreover, raptors serve as bellwethers of environmental change. Not only are they particularly vulnerable to environmental degradation, but they are conspicuous and fairly easy to monitor. For these reasons, conservationists devote particular attention to studying the population biology of raptors.

Many factors act independently and in concert to influence population size and density in birds of prey. Two of the most important factors influencing Red-tailed Hawk populations are nest site availability and food supply. The number and distribution of adequate nest sites directly affect reproductive effort, and food supply directly affects reproductive effort, reproductive success, and survivorship. Even though red-tails may nest in a dizzying array of nest sites, including canyon walls, utility poles, billboards, skyscrapers, and many species of trees (alive or dead), they require the sites to be elevated above the surrounding terrain and in close proximity to open hunting ground.

In this case, the hunting ground includes Central Park in New York City. Where appropriate sites are scarce, so are nesting red-tails, no matter how abundant the food supply. Conversely, nesting red-tails may be scarce in areas with plentiful nest sites if food availability is low. Even if a pair of red-tails attempts to nest in an area with a limited food supply, the chances of successfully raising a family are diminished. Where nesting sites and food supply are plentiful, nesting density may be limited by territorial behavior. In optimal areas, nesting densities may approach or even exceed one nesting pair per half a square mile (about 1.5 square kilometers) of suitable habitat.

As with most birds of prey, the Red-tailed Hawk is a relatively long-lived species. Generally, large raptors live longer than smaller ones. There is not enough information available to determine the maximum or average life span of a red-tail in the wild, but banding records provide some anecdotal information. The oldest red-tail recorded from band recoveries was more than twenty-three years old. In captivity, one red-tail lived past the age of twenty-nine years. By comparison, the oldest ages recorded for captive American Kestrels and Golden Eagles are seventeen and forty-six years, respectively.

The first year of life in the wild is typically the most difficult for any raptor to survive. Between one-half and two-thirds of Red-tailed Hawks hatched in a given year will not survive a full year in the wild. Thereafter, the average annual mortality rate is estimated (from very limited information) to be about 20 percent. Thus, out of a hundred red-tails hatched in a given year, assuming a 20 percent mortality rate after the first year, only between three and seven birds would be expected to reach ten years of age.

For a population to remain stable over time, the average number of young produced (or recruited) annually must equal the average number of individuals lost annually. When production exceeds loss, the population increases, and when loss exceeds production, the population declines.

In recent decades, the Red-tailed Hawk has expanded its range and increased in abundance in much of North America. Habitat alteration is a major reason for the decline in many raptor and other wildlife species. Red-tails, however, have benefited from habitat alteration, often at the expense of other species, such as Ferruginous and Red-shouldered hawks. Forest thinning in the East and fire suppression in the West have created wooded parkland habitats that provide attractive and productive nesting and hunting areas for red-tails.

Another reason for the increase in the red-tail population is the reduction in direct persecution by shooting, trapping, and poisoning. Through the first half of this century, raptors were seen as varmints, competing with human hunters for prized game species, such as quail and pheasant, and preying on domestic poultry. Red-tails are particularly vulnerable to shooting due to their habit of perching in the open. In many regions, the "chicken hawk" was shot whenever encountered, as a matter of civic responsibility.

Thousands of red-tails and other raptors were shot during migration as they passed near lookout points such as Kittatinny Ridge in Pennsylvania. Bounties were even offered for some raptor species, and to many people, the only good raptor was a dead raptor. But by the 1930s, conservationists had begun to speak out in earnest against the wanton slaughter of raptors. They mounted a campaign to institute legal protection for all birds of prey. Education was the most effective weapon in the conservationists' arsenal. As people learned more about the food habits of various raptors, many species began to be viewed as beneficial to farmers and to society at large. The Red-tailed Hawk was among those recognized as a beneficial species because of its habit of preying on rats, rabbits, and other potentially crop-damaging species.

Old attitudes and traditions die slowly, however. When I was growing up in the 1950s and early 1960s, it was common to see dead owls and hawks, including red-tails, displayed as trophies on rural fences. (The photo above was taken in northern Kentucky in the 1960s.) Although Bald and Golden eagles were granted explicit legal protection by the Bald Eagle Protection Act of 1940, it was not until 1972 that all native migratory birds, including birds of prey, received legal protection across the United States.

In spite of the fact that it is now against federal law to kill, injure, or harass any raptor in the United States, some hawks and eagles are illegally shot, trapped, or poisoned each year. Well-publicized cases over the past two decades have involved ranchers hiring shooters to kill eagles in the western United States and gamekeepers killing a variety of raptor species on a private estate in the southeastern United States. There is currently a fairly large, illegal trade in raptor feathers and other body parts for use in fabricating Indian artifacts. Indians can obtain permits to legally hold such parts and products for religious purposes, but poaching by both Indians and non-Indians still occurs. Eagle parts are generally most prized by poachers, but red-tail parts, especially the bright red tail feathers of adults, are frequently marketed. Because it is usually impossible to determine whether a feather, talon, or other part was taken from a murdered bird or simply found lying on the ground, mere possession of body parts is illegal without the appropriate permits.

Widespread chemical contamination from pesticides has never posed the threat to Red-tailed Hawk populations that it has to other species such as the Bald Eagle, Osprey, and Peregrine Falcon. Pesticides pose the greatest threat to species that feed at the top of long food chains, usually including other carnivores. At each level of the food chain, toxins in the pesticides become increasingly concentrated, so predators at the end of a long food chain accumulate large doses of the toxins. This process is termed biological magnification. The Bald Eagle, for example, is at the end of a very long food chain that might include, in addition to the large fish eaten directly by the eagle, smaller fish eaten by the large fish, invertebrates eaten by the smaller fish, plankton eaten by the invertebrates, and so on.

The red-tail, by contrast, is at the end of a relatively short food chain, often involving only an herbivore, such as a vole, that feeds directly on plant material. Although some DDT by-products and other toxic chemicals are ingested by red-tails, concentrations are usually too low to exert any toxic effects.

The remarkable morphological variation, behavioral flexibility, and ecological tolerance exhibited by the Red-tailed Hawk provide it with important tools that help it survive, and even thrive, in an ever-changing world. Some of the profound alterations brought about by one of the planet's most important purveyors of change—humankind—have actually enhanced this adaptable raptor's place in its homeland. Due to its dietary versatility, it can respond opportunistically to fluctuations among many different prey populations.

Because of its broad range of nest sites, it can reproduce in a wide array of situations. It is also well suited, by virtue of its position at the end of a relatively short food chain, to withstand widespread environmental chemical contamination.

Thus, like a good utility infielder, the versatile red-tail can thrive in a number of difficult situations that we create for it. If any raptor—indeed, any wild predator—is capable of withstanding the continued onslaught of human-induced change in North America, the Red-tailed Hawk is a good bet to endure, and perhaps to inspire our descendants to contemplate a time and a world less tame than their own.

Selected References

Bent, A. C. 1937. *Life Histories of North American Birds of Prey.* Vol. 1. Washington, DC: United States National Museum. Reprint ed., New York: Dover Publishing, 1961.

Brett, J. J. 1986. *The Mountain and the Migration.* Kutztown, PA: Hawk Mountain Sanctuary.

Brown, L., and D. Amadon. 1968. *Eagles, Hawks, and Falcons of the World.* New York: McGraw-Hill.

Craighead, J. J., and F. C. Craighead, Jr. 1956. *Hawks, Owls, and Wildlife.* Harrisburg, PA: Stackpole Books. Reprint ed., New York: Dover Publishing, 1969.

Fitch, H. S., F. Swenson, and D. F. Tillotson. 1946. Behavior and food habits of the Red-tailed Hawk. *Condor* 48:205–257.

Henny, C. J., and H. M. Wight. 1972. Population ecology and environmental pollution: Red-tailed and Cooper's Hawks. Pp. 229–250 in *Population Ecology of Migratory Birds: A Symposium.* Wildlife Research Report 2. Washington, DC: U.S. Department of Interior.

Houston, C. S., and M. J. Bechard. 1983. Red-tailed Hawk distribution, Saskatchewan. *Blue Jay* 41:99–109.

Johnsgard, P. A. 1990. *Hawks, Eagles and Falcons of North America.* Washington, DC: Smithsonian Institution Press.

Johnson, S. J. 1986. Development of hunting and self-sufficiency in juvenile Red-tailed Hawks *(Buteo jamaicensis). Raptor Research* 20:29–34.

Kerlinger, P. 1989. *Flight Strategies of Migrating Hawks.* Chicago: University of Chicago Press.

Knight, R. L., and A. W. Erickson. 1976. High incidence of snakes in the diet of nesting Red-tailed Hawks. *Raptor Research* 10:108–111.

Mader, W. J. 1978. A comparative nesting study of Red-tailed Hawks and Harris Hawks in southern Arizona. *Auk* 95:327–337.

Moritsch, M. Q. 1983. *Photographic Guide for Aging Nestling Red-tailed Hawks.* Boise, ID: U.S. Department of Interior Bureau of Land Management.

Newton, I. 1979. *Population Ecology of Raptors.* Vermillion, SD: Buteo Books.

Newton, I., and P. Olsen, eds. 1990. *Birds of Prey.* New York: Facts on File.

Palmer, R. S., ed. 1988. *Handbook of North American Birds.* Vol. 5. New Haven, CT: Yale University Press.

Preston, C. R. 1980. Differential perch site selection by color morphs of the Red-tailed Hawk *(Buteo jamaicensis). Auk* 97:782–789.

——·1990. Distribution of raptor foraging in relation to prey biomass and habitat structure. *Condor* 92:107–112.

Preston, C. R., and R. D. Beane. 1993. The Red-tailed Hawk. In *The Birds of North America,* no. 52, edited by A. Poole and F. Gill. Philadelphia: Academy of Natural Sciences; Washington, DC: American Ornithologists' Union.

Root, T. 1988. *Atlas of Wintering North American Birds: An Analysis of Christmas Bird Count Data.* Chicago: University of Chicago Press.

Snyder, N. F. R., and H. A. Snyder. 1991. *Birds of Prey: Natural History and Conservation of North American Raptors.* Stillwater, MN: Voyageur Press.

Voelker, T. 1969. Mating behavior of Red-tailed Hawks. *Loon* 41:90–91.

Weidensaul, S. 1996. *Raptors: The Birds of Prey.* New York: Lyons & Burford.

Wheeler, B. K., and W. S. Clark. 1995. *A Photographic Guide to North American Raptors.* San Diego, CA: Academic Press.

Wildon, P. W., and E. M. Grigsby. 1979. Combined nesting of Red-tailed Hawks and House Sparrows. *International Bird Banding* 51:75.

Wiley, J. W. 1975. Three adult Red-tailed Hawks tending a nest. *Condor* 77:480–482.

Winn, M. 1998. *Red-Tails in Love: A Wildlife Drama in Central Park.* New York: Pantheon Books.

Photo Credits

Page 1
Russ Kerr

Page 2
Ron Austing

Page 3
Richard Day/Daybreak
Imagery (top)
Ron Austing (bottom)

Page 4
Robert McCaw (top)
Jim Roetzel (bottom)

Page 5
Ron Austing (top)
Robert McCaw
(bottom left)
Jeffrey Rich Nature
Photography
(bottom right)

Page 6
D. Robert Franz

Page 7
Curt Given

Page 8
Jeffrey Rich Nature
Photography (top)
Tom Vezo (bottom)

Page 9
Ron Austing (top)
Richard Day/Daybreak
Imagery (bottom)

Page 10
Ron Austing (top)
Richard Day/Daybreak
Imagery (bottom left)
Tom J. Ulrich
(bottom right)

Page 11
Jim Roetzel (top)
Russ Kerr (bottom)

Page 12
Wayne Lynch (left
and right top)
Russ Kerr (left and
right bottom)

Page 13
D. Dvorak Jr. (left)
Laura Riley (right)

Page 14
Richard Day/Daybreak
Imagery (top and
bottom)

Page 15
Kit Breen

Page 16
Ron Austing (left
and right)

Page 17
D. Dvorak Jr.

Page 18
Richard Day/Daybreak
Imagery (top)
D. Dvorak Jr. (bottom)

Page 19
Tom J. Ulrich

Page 20
Deborah Allen (top
and bottom)

Page 21
Deborah Allen

Page 22
Russ Kerr

Page 23
Tom J. Ulrich (left)
John Cancalosi (right)

Page 24
Deborah Allen

Page 25
Cary C. Given

Page 26
Tom J. Ulrich

Page 27
Deborah Allen (top)
Ron Austing (middle)
Deborah Allen (bottom)

Page 28
Russ Kerr

Page 29
Russ Kerr

Page 30
Tom J. Ulrich

Page 31
Gregory K. Scott

Page 32
John Cancalosi

Page 33
Ron Austing (top)
Deborah Allen (bottom)

Page 34
Russ Kerr

Page 35
Russ Kerr

Page 36
Tom Vezo

Page 37
Wayne Lynch

Page 38
Ron Austing

Page 39
Ron Austing

Page 40
Ron Austing

Page 41
Ron Austing

Page 42
John Cancalosi

Page 43
John Cancalosi

Page 44
Ron Austing

Page 45
John Cancalosi (top
and bottom)

Page 46
Ron Austing

Page 47
Ron Austing

Page 48
Ron Austing

Page 49
Russ Kerr

Page 50
Russ Kerr (top and
bottom)

Page 51
John Cancalosi (top)
Deborah Allen (bottom)

Page 52
John Cancalosi

Page 53
Jeffrey Rich (left)
Laura Riley (right)

Page 54
Russ Kerr (top and
bottom)

Page 55
Deborah Allen (top
and bottom)

Page 56
Deborah Allen

Page 57
Deborah Allen

Page 58
Deborah Allen

Page 59
Deborah Allen

Page 60
Tom J. Ulrich

Page 61
Cliff Beittel

Page 62
Ron Austing

Page 63
Richard Day/Daybreak
  Imagery

Page 64
D. Dvorak Jr.

Page 65
Curt Given

Page 66
Deborah Allen

Page 67
Tom Vezo

Page 68
Robert McCaw

Page 69
Tom Vezo

Page 70
D. Dvorak Jr.

Page 71
Deborah Allen (top)
Richard Day/Daybreak
  Imagery (bottom)

Page 72
Deborah Allen (left)
Richard Day/Daybreak
  Imagery (right)

Page 74
Robert McCaw

Page 75
Tom Vezo (top)
Deborah Allen (bottom)

Page 76
Curt Given (top)
Deborah Allen (bottom)

Page 77
Deborah Allen (top)
Tom J. Ulrich (bottom)

Page 78
Deborah Allen

Page 79
Charles W. Melton

Page 80
Jeffrey Rich Nature
  Photography

Page 81
Deborah Allen

Page 82
Tom J. Ulrich

Page 83
Wayne Lynch

Page 84
Jim Roetzel

Page 85
Tom Vezo (top)
John Cancalosi
  (bottom)

Page 86
Deborah Allen

Page 87
Deborah Allen

Page 88
Gregory K. Scott

Page 89
Ron Austing

Page 90
Cary C. Given

Page 91
Deborah Allen

Page 92
John Cancalosi (left)
Kit Breen (right)

Page 93
Russ Kerr (left)
Deborah Allen (right)

Page 94
Jeffrey Rich Nature
  Photography

About the Author

Charles R. Preston is curator of natural history at the Buffalo Bill Historical Center in Cody, Wyoming. He is a former chairman of zoology and curator of ornithology at the Denver Museum of Natural History and associate professor of biology at the University of Arkansas, Little Rock. He has written numerous articles on the Red-tailed Hawk and other birds of prey for scientific journals and popular publications. He and his wife live in a cabin overlooking the North Fork of the Shoshone River in Wyoming.

Index